GHOSTS
OF
BORDENTOWN

guy arlen publishing LLC
2005

GHOSTS
OF
BORDENTOWN

Arlene S. Bice

guy arlen publishing LLC

Dedication

This book is dedicated to my sons
Kenny, Bret, Guy, and Ralph Morrison.
They grew up with tunnels in their basement.

Table of Contents

Acknowledgements

First, many thanks to the courageous people who stepped up and told their stories to me. Courageous because they ignored those who would laugh and they disregarded the non-believers. They gave me permission to share these stories with the public. Of this, I am grateful. Please respect their privacy.

Secondly, many thanks to Hannelore Hahn, founder of the International Women Writers' Guild and to its members. They are the women who lit my fire to follow my dream of becoming a published writer. The teachers guided, prodded, and encouraged, bringing forth memories I thought I had forgotten and sparked new ideas that I needed. Of this, I am also grateful.

Thirdly, many thanks to the wonderful people of Historical Bordentown City, NJ. They are always there when you need them the most.

Foreword

A visit brought me a day of beautiful visions of earlier inhabitants of Bordentown. Carriages, preparations for parties, a grieving family, a town filled with souls that embrace love—all these and so much more are vivid reminders of a stroll through Bordentown with Arlene Bice, an historian whose spiritual quests helped me put these images and feelings into a cohesive understanding of why Bordentown is unique.

Ghosts of Bordentown is, of course, a must for the metaphysically inclined. It is also a must read for anyone who cares to understand that not only does history repeat itself, but it can also repeat in a spiritual and loving manner as does Bordentown's populace today. By taking us through the web of lives that have been part of Bordentown's history and the loving acceptance of these spirits that still grace the town, Arlene Bice shows us the way to enlightenment.

May the Ghosts of Bordentown haunt us all, for that is how we will learn to build a world, home-by-home, town-by-town, state-by-state, and country-by-country. –Nancy Orlen Weber, Author of *Psychic Detective and The Gift of Interspecies Communication*

Introduction

For several years, I conducted a Ghost Walk for my business group, the Downtown Bordentown Association, as a fundraiser. It was an evening of entertainment with gifted storytellers in front of each house on the tour telling the tale in their own words. But the stories were true. At first, it was difficult. There were only a few stories available. But soon, people realized they wouldn't be laughed at; that others had similar stories of their own to share. Then folks started to drift into my gift/bookshop one at a time to tell me of their experience.

The day after the tour took place, I could always count on visitors in my shop, asking questions about hauntings, psychics, poltergeists, phenomena, and did I have something they could take away, such as a flier or sheet of information. Out of those requests came the idea to finally put some of those wonderful stories in written form.

Ghosts can be elusive creatures. One family can live in a house for a generation or two and never have an inkling that they have a resident ghost. When the house is sold, another family moves in, and wow! They see ghosts that have inhabited the house for a century.

There are reasons for this. Some people are more open and receptive to the 'sixth sense.' It's been said that we all have extrasensory perception, but some of us develop it more than others. My grandmother, Elizabeth Urbanski Daniels, was born with a veil on her face and fully developed psychic abilities. My mother, Anna Mae Bice Riggi, had extraordinary psychic abilities where her children were concerned. I've had moments throughout my life when I was fully aware of my psychic abilities.

My son Kenny came racing into the kitchen one hot summer afternoon. He was about 6 years old. "Mommy, Daddy's on fire!" I knew his father was in the bedroom sleeping. To reassure him that everything was okay, I took him by the hand to peek into the bedroom. To my surprise, the electric extension cord to the air conditioner was sparking flames! Surely, my son saved his father's life.

Ghosts have been known to remain with a building, a property, or to follow along with a member of the household when they move to another location. They often seem to have a strong tie, a 'bonded' effect to whatever or whomever they have attached themselves. Turmoil can be a cause for spirits to not want to move on to the next plane, to remain here until their personal situation is resolved. The recorded past of Bordentown has revealed unsettled times.

History sets in Bordentown like a shawl on an old woman's shoulders, starting with the Revolutionary War. The town was full of patriots willing to act upon their plans for liberty. Their sense of justice and loyalty to their own beliefs got them into trouble more than once. The British and Hessians occupied the town. Houses were burned, looted, and people attacked, some killed.

In the 19th century, Irish immigrants dug the D & R Canal starting here in Bordentown. They were imported for that very purpose. America's railroads in steam began here, where Bordentown was also reputed to operate a different kind of railroad—the 'underground railroad'—before and during the Civil War period. Many houses had a hidden room tucked away somewhere unexpected. Some had a secret tunnel under the house. Both periods of time had emotions, beliefs, and patriotism running strong and deep.

In the years that I've been interviewing and listening to the tales of the supernatural in Bordentown, I haven't heard of any stories about our spirits being evil or vindictive. One spirit definitely made his opinion known, but then another spirit actually saved the lives of an entire family. Their stories are told here.

To protect the privacy of our generous witnesses to the ghostly happenings of Bordentown, I've used only first names and general areas. The book was written for you to enjoy, and I hope you do so. Remember, if you decide to go ghost hunting, walk lightly, and keep in mind that many ghosts are lost, kind, and gentle spirits.

Enjoy,

Arlene S. Bice

Jackie's Story

The Herron family resided in Bordentown in the late 1800s. When their son, Dr. John Herron, married, he purchased the property next door to his mother with plans to raise his family and to house his veterinary practice. After his parents died, his sister remained in the family home and raised her family there. A few generations of the same family were connected to these two properties.

In 1969, the widow of Dr. John sold the property and moved to California to be with her daughter. A few years later, the Herron descendants relocated locally and rented their home to a young couple.

It wasn't long before the young couple turned into a family of three. Late one night, the new mother went down to the kitchen to warm a bottle for her baby. She ascended the stairs to return to her child's room on the second floor when she saw an apparition of an old woman in a white nightgown at the top of the stairs. The mother screamed and ran from the house looking for help.

The next day, she sought the aid of a parapsychologist from Princeton University who inspected the house and agreed that the property was, indeed, haunted. The young family left the house immediately, never to return.

My family lived next door. We considered the episode a colorful story, but a story, nonetheless—until a year later.

In our house, my family was also a young one. In the middle of a winter night, a gentle nudging of my shoulder awakened me. Opening my eyes, I saw an apparition of a short woman in a white nightgown with a high ruffled collar and the appearance of curlers rolled in her hair. The figure stood by the side of my bed for a brief time and then moved swiftly across the room and out the door. I climbed out of bed and followed her into the hall. Smoke! The strong smell of smoke was in the hallway! I raced down the stairs to the kitchen where I found a pan on the stove ablaze. My brother had fallen asleep after attempting to warm some leftovers. My husband and I extinguished the fire. Then I told him of the woman in a white nightgown. He excused it as an intuitive dream.

The eerie experience piqued my curiosity. I spoke to one of the Herrons' grandchildren who still lived in the area. The description of the old woman matched that of the grandmother who always wore her hair in tight curls piled on top of her head. She died in the very room that she appeared in.

We stayed and raised our children in the house, but other occurrences did take place. At times, guests also had ghostly experiences. The strangest, however, was the appearance of an old woman seated at the dinner table with our family in a photograph taken with a new Polaroid camera. There had been no old woman invited to dinner that night!

More recently, with our first grandchild here and two more expected, the cradle in the corner of the room rocks, ever so gently—and no hand can be seen touching it.

Mary's Story

I don't know who my resident ghosties were, but they made the best smelling French roast coffee that you can imagine. The aroma of that coffee and slightly burnt toast would permeate my second floor apartment. This was shortly after I moved in. I lived alone. Well, at least you couldn't see anyone else that was living there. After many years at this address, my mother, now deceased, came to live with me. The coffee aroma intrigued her to the point that she finally spoke to the landlord about it.

"Ray, what brand of coffee do you make every night at 11 o'clock?"

"I use the same brand of coffee you do, Rose. You know that, and what would I be doing making coffee that late at night, anyway?" He paused, looked at her strangely, "I thought that was you making coffee."

There were very strong aromas throughout the day that couldn't be accounted for. Around 4:30–5:30 in the early evening, the strong smell of a hard workingman's perspiration floated through the air, as if a man had just come home from a hard laboring job and headed for the bath to clean up. About 30 minutes later, the air would be filled with the wonderful aroma of a cherry-blend pipe tobacco. A wonderful, pleasant aroma. The landlord didn't smoke.

During the winter months when the house was all closed up, the light floral scent of camellias wafted through the air. It just freshened up the atmosphere.

Another strange incident occurred. Coming home from work one day, I parked my car and entered the backyard approaching the stairs that led to my apartment. I noticed there was a blue light emanating from my windows, a vivid cobalt blue light. The blue light was filling my kitchen. I stopped and stared because I have no blue bulbs anywhere in my apartment. I walked very quietly towards the house, hoping to get closer to the kitchen door, where I might be able to see what was causing the light. However, before I was able to get 3 feet from the stairs, the light vanished. Of course, no one was there when I entered.

Another incident happened, and this one was very annoying. Things are not where I left them; for example, when I laid clothes out over my kitchen chair that I was going to wear to work. I took a shower, went to the kitchen to slip into my clothes, the slacks were there; the shirt was gone. No one was in my apartment. I looked under the chair, under the table, mumbled some savory oaths, looked in my bedroom. Couldn't find my shirt anywhere. Finally, I found another shirt and went to work. Two months later, I found my shirt under the dust ruffle of my bed! It hadn't been there the day before.

There was a time when I had been having problems with wasps in the apartment. One night, I was lying in bed reading. I was very jumpy, just waiting for the next wasp to fly through. Something, a movement caught my eye. I was feeling brave with paperback book in hand, knowing this wasp was going to meet his maker soon.

I put the book in my right hand. I was ready; I was going to get this bugger. However, when I looked up into the hallway at my bedroom doorway, the movement was not a wasp. It was a small, slightly built man with gray hair, a dark kind of 'Abe Lincoln' type suit with celluloid collar on his shirt. And I could see through him! He was all in black and white, and I could see through him! He was walking down the hall towards the other end of the house. His head was bowed. There was an air of sadness about him. And I could see right through him! I started to get out of bed to confront him and poof—he was gone. I truly believe he was the previous owner of the house, the one whose estate sold the house to my present landlord.

I guess the most interesting incident was the earring. My landlord was sitting at his desk in the dining room writing out checks to pay his bills. He was grumbling to himself about the taxes being increased, along with everything else, about how tough it was making ends meet.

All of a sudden, he felt something hit him in the head. Whatever it was, it slid down off his shoulder, onto his lap, then to the floor. Now, the man was stunned. He lived alone. No one else was in the apartment. He bent down to pick up the item. It was a woman's earring! He was dumbfounded.

When I got home from work, my telephone was ringing demandingly. At least it seemed so. I picked up the phone.
"Mary, it's Ray. Would you come downstairs please?"

I arrived to see a very pale Ray. He handed me an earring. "Is this yours? Did you lose this?"

I looked at it, shook my head. I had never seen it before.

"Could it have been entangled in the laundry, or could I have stood too close to someone at the market and gotten it caught on my shirt? Or could it have fallen through the floor from your apartment to mine?"

"It's not mine, Ray." Then he told me exactly what had happened. This time I was stunned.

He handed me the earring. "You can have it. If the other one shows up, you'll have a pair."

I took the earring to the jeweler in town, who identified it as mid-to-late 1800s costume jewelry. I told Ray the incident reminded me of Elizabeth Taylor's ad for her White Diamonds perfume. "She gave one of her earrings to a man who was short of money at the gaming table. Only she handed him the earring. She didn't smack him on the top of the head with it."

Mimi's Story

As a promising, handsome, energetic young man, devoted to his father, J. Turner Brakeley faced a future of being a great barrister. When he was approximately 25 years of age, he fell deeply in love with a student at the Bordentown Female College. His father, Reverend Brakeley, was superintendent of this college, located across the street from their home.

J. Turner and the young lady were betrothed and would set a date to be married as soon as he established himself in the business of the law—but it was not to be.

Only once did he speak of the incident that changed his life forever. He confided to his laundress, Mrs. Embley of New Egypt.

"He spoke softly," Mrs. Emley told of the time they talked, "almost reluctantly. And he never did mention her name."

"I broke the engagement." He still looked very broken-hearted. "I was coming up the stairs in my home in Bordentown when I came upon her in the arms of another man. A strange quirk, I never would have seen her but for the mirror, a long mirror standing at an angle at the top of the stairs showing the reflection of her in his arms. A mirror, like a camera, does not lie."

"Oh, there were offers of apologies, explanations, and pleas. But my dream was shattered. My ideals were too high, my faith damaged. I never wanted to see her or any other woman in my life.

I decided to leave the area and live alone." He was unaware of the deep sigh that left him looking still very melancholy after all the years that had passed.

"I soon informed my father of my decision. He was very disappointed at my choice of a future. Indeed, I think I broke his heart as well."

J. Turner moved to La-Ha-Way, the house deep in the pinelands that his father also owned. Taking just a few personal belongings, he maintained a neat, well-kept appearance. He excluded most people from his life, studied cranberry plants and flowers, bees, and birds, keeping meticulous records. He studied the winds, stars, trees, and insects. Some called him a poet.

In 1912, he became ill, returned to Bordentown, and died.

The house in Bordentown that the Reverend Brakeley owned, across from the Female College, was bought and sold a few times after J. Turner's death. He had refused to live in it or anywhere else other than the pinelands.

My husband and I saw the house and felt it was perfect for us. We had plans of painting and fixing it to put our touch in it. As soon as we moved in, a strange phenomena began. The telephone rang at 11:00 every night. No one was ever at the other end of the line.

Linesmen came to the house to search for a reason. Workmen looked over the house seeking a cause for the ringing. The telephone company came to the house and checked all the wiring. Finally, a new telephone was installed. Still, at 11:00 p.m., the telephone rang. We never could find an explanation for it. We just adapted to the fact that the telephone was going to ring. And it did. On schedule. Every night.

We continued our restoration of the house. We turned one of the rooms upstairs into a feminine little playroom for our daughter. In the process, we removed the long mirror and the telephone from the top of the stairs to another area of the house. The telephone was silent at 11:00 at night.

We wonder, was it the lovely fiancée with yet another explanation? Or J. Turner with a sad story to tell his father? It seems the removal of the long mirror; a source of pain and anguish for J. Turner, now allows him to rest in peace.

Jane's Story

When we were still a young married couple and living in this house in Bordentown City, my husband and I noticed the lights going on and off with no one turning the switch. This happened often, with the two of us sitting there and no one else near. We looked at each other, not knowing what to say. From time-to-time, we felt a coldness about us, especially going up the stairs—the coldness would follow right on up with you. There was no draft from anywhere, and it didn't feel like a draft kind of coldness anyway. It was different, just this 'coldness' hanging about you. We couldn't imagine an explanation for it.

As time went by, our daughter chose the third floor for her bedroom. "Mom! Where's my jewelry box? Why do you move my things around?" My daughter would be yelling but, of course, I hadn't even been in her room. She thought I was snooping in her room because this would happen often with different trinkets of hers.

Many times, I heard footsteps in the hall or on the stairway, but when I looked, no one was there. That was the area we mostly felt the cold air or heard the sounds of someone walking.

I became pregnant with my son and, one night, early morning, really, I got up out of bed to go to the bathroom. I groggily reached in to feel for the light switch—and—standing right there, a really tall man, arms folded across his chest. He had a long pointed beard and he was wearing an old-time sailor's suit. A very stern expression covered his face.

I ran back into my bedroom and awakened my husband, Joe. He grumbled, but got up and checked the bathroom—nothing! No one!

I have never seen him since that early morning. That was a long time ago now. It's as if he were just letting me know that he was there. The lights work now, as they are supposed to work, and the coldness is gone. Things aren't moved around either. They stay where they are placed in any area of the house.

A neighbor, May, remembered that when she was a little girl, a really long time ago (she was about 90 years old when we spoke), a man hanged himself in this house. I'm still researching to find who it was and what happened here.

Jim's Story

This building, Riverview Studios, overlooks Crosswicks Creek where the creek enters the Delaware River. The Lenape Tribes fished and camped along here before the Europeans moved in. In Revolutionary War times, ships sailed up the Crosswicks to hide from British warships. Some did not sail back down again. Their wooden ribs stick out of the marsh in low tide. In the next century, Joseph Bonaparte used this creek to transport goods and treasures brought to his estate, Pointe Breeze. He built secret tunnels that led from his house to his daughter's house and to the creek.

When I'm standing in front of my studio facing the creek, on the right of the building, is a long, severe flight of concrete stairs that descend from Hilltop Park. Those with extra sensitivity say that a 'heaviness,' a foreboding, is in the air here. That feeling seems to be stronger between the end of summer through April.

To the far right of the bottom of those stairs is a tumbled pile of tombstones dumped by someone who didn't seem to care. Some of the dates are as recent as 1920. Portions of the stones, still readable, reveal the names of Florence Purcell, a little girl who died from lockjaw resulting from a splinter. Another is Phoebe L. Taylor, Louisa Amelia Ramond, or Ramono. Ferry is also a name found on a chunk of granite.

A century ago, St. Mary's Church cemetery was located above us on the bluff. We wonder if the stones belonged there at one time.

In front, but off to the right of the building, is a railroad trestle crossing the creek where the train heads for Trenton. Over the long years, since the railroad started here in Bordentown, many people have jumped to their death from that trestle.

Bordering my property, on the left, is the road climbing steeply upward turning into Farnsworth Avenue. This area, from the bottom of the hill to about half way up, is haunted. At dusk, a wall of shadows floats across the rising road. A gloom permeates the air. The sensitive ones feel moodiness, anger, even hatred lying there. Not everyone can walk up the hill at dusk. Driving up is no problem. But walking is another matter.

My block and stucco building sets on the flat portion of land backing up to the bluff. This was formerly the Riverview Iron Works built in 1888. J. Holmes Longstreet brought it into importance by the turn of the century. They boasted of the latest mechanical appliances known to the industry. Marine stationary engines, rotary pumps, castings, and specialty items were turned. Match machines and sand dredgers were made under the careful eye of Mr. Al T. Thompson, superintendent. Up to 20 handpicked expert mechanics were employed, along with other skilled workmen.

It stood empty for several years before we came along. In order to refurbish the building, there was a tremendous amount of work ahead of us. Inside the building, we manually sandblasted the old stucco to reveal the beauty of the original brickwork. While we worked with hammer and chisel, paint and brush, many people stopped by with their stories. Telling us their personal histories as their eyes sparkled bringing life into their faces also brought life into the building's story. The re-telling of what they knew to be true. Interesting memories of old timers.

My son Christopher was a teenager then. He worked side-by-side with me on the building. Once in August, nearing midnight, he was finishing the cleanup from the day's work. He heard a thump, thought it was me, but saw no one when he looked around. Silence followed, so he paid no more attention to it. Some time later, he heard it again, like someone walking up the stairs to the loft of the building. Again, no one was seen. From that time, the 'walking up the stairs' was heard whenever someone was working late. It continued throughout the remaining summer. Doors opened and closed without a visible hand on the doorknobs. Everyone attributed it the wind or 'something.'

After a few weeks of the unexplained sounds, Christopher set up a recording tape to run through the night. Beginning at 11:30, footsteps came down the stairs slowly. At 12:45, the door slams. It opens and closes with a slam when no one is there. Yet the door remained locked as we left it.

In mid-September, near dusk, Christopher headed for the roadway. He reached about 30 feet from the bottom when this intense fear came over him. The hairs on his arms and neck stood on end. He tilted his head down and started to run up the hill. Bump! "My foot hit something solid! Big black work shoes. I looked up and saw this man, over 6 feet in height. He wore a black bowler hat. He was thin, tall with a strong fierce look about him. I looked down to his shoes again. As suddenly as he appeared, when I looked up, he was gone. After that, I took the stairs up the hill."

People continued to stop by to chat while we carried on our work. One old-timer brought us photos of the place when it was Riverview Iron Works. Chris recognized one man in a bowler hat to be the man he bumped into on the hill. The photo was probably taken around 1900. On another day, a guy visiting the area stopped down to see the old place. He said, when the building was a foundry, early in the 1900s, the owner hired a man afflicted with Tourette's syndrome. Local youths taunted him unmercifully. He retaliated by coming out and throwing tools at them. Despite these difficulties and because the man was a good worker, Mr. Longstreet also allowed the man to live there at night. In this way, he doubled as a night watchman.

Christopher has not seen him since we completed the restoration to the original appearance of the building. The sounds on the stairs continue, though, with decreasing frequency.

The wall of shadows on the road up the hill is as strong as ever.

Juanita's Story

My good friend, the late Juanita, was tall, slender, and had flaming red hair. Her appearance, with the bright colors she always wore, was an indication of her vibrant personality. She was a talented, well-known artist and probably taught art to someone from every household in Bordentown City. In 1986, she bought the old 1886 Citizen's Hook & Ladder Firehouse on Walnut Street and turned it into her residence, studio, and classroom. Everyone knew and adored Juanita.

At times, we would go out for a martini and dinner. She would reminisce about her youth. This is her story.

"My mother died while I was still very young. My father worked odd and long hours on the railroad. My brother was several years younger, so it was my responsibility to look after him. Sometimes we would stay in town with my mother's parents and sometimes we walked out into the country to stay with my father's parents."

At this point, Juanita paused, looking into the distant past that I couldn't see. But I knew she was looking at scenes from her childhood, so different from the other kids that she knew. She continued.

"My father's mother was a plain, hard-working woman and tried her best to make me into that image also. No silliness or frilliness was allowed when we were there. But, when I came into town, my mother's mother would dress me with bangles, bracelets, and brightly colored clothes. There would be music in the house and a lot of laughter.

In the spring and summer when we were in town, she would always warn us to stay away from the gypsies that camped on Mill Street along the edge of the woods. I snuck up close enough to peek at their bright dresses, belts, and the bandannas they wore on their heads. I could hear their tambourines release music into the air while they danced around the campfire. They didn't seem at all dangerous, but I didn't get too close either.

The only part of staying at the house in town that I didn't like was when she sent me to the basement for potatoes, onions, or whatever was in cold storage. I always felt creepy down there. I really, really hated it, but didn't want to admit that I was frightened.

When I finally told this to Grandma, she showed me a spot in the dirt basement that never dried. No matter what she did, this 'wet' spot would always return. Time and again she tried to remove it to no avail. The kitchen door that led to the basement was troublesome also. It would spring open. Even when it was locked, something would pop that lock and it would stand ajar. I thought it was Grandpa playing a trick on me. But it happened when he wasn't there. Grandma didn't seem to worry about it, but it worried me. It was the strangest thing.

Later, I was told that a carpenter committed suicide by cutting his throat and his wrists. Then he managed to hang himself. All this took place on a peaceful Sunday morning in the basement of my grandma's house where he lived with his ailing sister many years before my Grandpa bought the house. He was out of work for some time and became very despondent. The man was a pleasant person, respected, and liked by his neighbors and friends. So tragic. Now that I look back, I think he left his mark on the house with that wet spot. I also think that his spirit changed its mind and was trying to come back into the warm kitchen."

The Author's Story

It's been said often enough that we all have psychic abilities, that some people are more developed in that way than others. My grandmother, Elizabeth Urbanski Daniels, was born with a veil on her face and fully developed psychic abilities. My mother, Anna Mae Bice Riggi, had extraordinary psychic abilities where her children were concerned. I've had moments throughout my life when I was fully aware of my psychic abilities.

My son Kenny came racing into the kitchen one hot summer afternoon. He was about 6 years old. "Mommy, Daddy's on fire!" I knew his father was in the bedroom sleeping. To reassure him that everything was okay, I took him by the hand to peek into the bedroom. To my surprise, the electric extension cord to the air conditioner was sparking flames! Surely, my son saved his father's life.

Several years later, my marriage crumbled into a battleground. In the middle of the night, I left my husband of 15 years and took my four sons and my widowed mother with me. I went directly to my bachelor brother's apartment and began to plan for a future.

First, he helped me get a job. Then he helped me to locate a house. I was determined to live in Bordentown, especially for the excellent school system. These were not easy to do, considering my lack of a high school diploma or a credit history in my own name. This was the early 1970s, when the average woman rarely got credit on her own merit.

The newness of my employment was also a factor. Each weekend, we looked at houses in the price range I could afford on my new salary. The location of the first one was ruled out. The second one was tiny and located next to a fire house—not suitable. The third didn't 'feel' right. The fourth needed too much work to be comfortable. An apartment was ruled out. No one would rent to me with four children. I was becoming dismayed. I couldn't impose on my brother's generosity much longer. Finally, someone told him of a house tucked away on a tiny side street in Bordentown City. It was the only house on the street. The location was perfect, away from the center of town, and a stone's throw from a forest and a creek. The home we left was also near a wooded area and the boys spent as much time there as they could manage.

My brother Bob contacted the real estate office and set up an appointment for early Saturday morning. We met the realtor at the house. We entered through the front door directly into the living room. It was small, but felt full of warmth. Straight ahead on the left were the steps to the second floor. Across the room on the right, I took a step down to a pleasant dining room. A door off to the right led to a screened-in porch. Across that room and another step down and I was in a large kitchen. Bright yellow. Not modern, but sufficient with lots of cabinets and scalloped woodwork trim. Beyond the kitchen, through a wide archway, was a dining cove wrapped with windows. The sun was bursting through the windows casting cheerfulness over the room, a promise of happiness. I just filled with joy picturing all of us around the table being a happy family again. I agreed right then and there to buy the house.

"This is it. This is home."

The sales person laughed. "You haven't seen the second and third floors yet."

"I don't have to, but to make you happy, let's go."

I looked at the front bedroom, which would be mine. The tiny closet was the old-fashioned kind where you had to hang your clothes on a peg. It was easy to see people didn't own much in the way of clothing when this house was built. Those were the days of a dress for Sunday and one for the week.

The two front windows overlooked the quiet street. A street not wide enough for two cars passing, one would have to back down the street. Two steps down into the back bedroom for the two younger boys. This also had a small closet. The bright sun shone through the large window that overlooked the roof of the breakfast room. Perfect for bunk beds. Along the interior wall was the stairway leading up to the third floor and a neat hide-a-way room. This had a sloping ceiling, giving it an interesting look. It reminded me of the attic in the house I grew up in, except it was a lot smaller. I loved that attic and now this one, too.

Mom would want the dining room converted to a bedroom. She wouldn't have to climb stairs for the bathroom located off the living room. That was a little inconvenient, but easy to live with. The rest fit perfectly.

The paperwork went smoothly. We settled in.

When I left my husband, I had only the clothes I was wearing. I had nothing else. Friends were very generous. They donated odd bits of furniture and furnishings to us, even books, toys, and clothes for the boys. I began to rebuild a life.

My newly acquired day job, working in an office Monday through Friday, paid the bills. On Friday and Saturday nights, when the boys were visiting their father, I tended bar at an old historic tavern in the countryside. This was for the extra money that was always needed. It was a busy schedule. The boys, ages 7 to 13 years old, were all in school. My mother was there to help out and was home when the boys came charging in the door, hungry, after a long day of being confined in a classroom.

On the weekend nights that I worked, I would get home about 3 o'clock in the morning and sometimes later. Tending a busy bar is no easy feat. And we were always busy. It was fun, too, but I was standing, and sometimes running, on a tiled concrete floor for 6 hours straight. Often under pressure, when the bar and dining room were packed with thirsty patrons. When I got home, sleep came quickly and soundly.

One Friday night–Saturday morning really, I awoke from a deep sleep. It must have been about 4 o'clock. Standing just inside my bedroom doorway was a little girl. She stood around 3 feet high and looked to be about 6 or 7 years old. Her hair was fair, long, and curling at the ends. She wore a floor-length nightdress and a nightcap with a ruffle around it. The candle she held flickered a bright flame. A pensive but pleasant expression on her face seemed to be telling me that she was checking out the new family now living in her home.

Without speaking a word, she conveyed a welcome to me. She approved. Then she just disappeared. Just faded away. Just dissolved.

I was bone tired. I was comforted. I fell back to sleep.

When I awoke the next morning, I thought of the little girl immediately, before I even placed my foot on the floor. I lay there thinking about her and decided not to say anything to my mom. I didn't want to frighten her or be ridiculed as to having a dream.

So I said nothing to anyone. After all, the appearance of a spirit in one's bedroom could be the beginning of a lot of innuendoes and jokes about my condition when I went to bed. I was tired, but I knew what I saw and I also knew that I didn't have to explain it to anyone else.

Mom's Story
(Refers to the Author's Story)

My mother, Elizabeth Urbanski Daniels, was born with a veil on her face. This means that a thin piece of skin covering her complete face at birth had to be cut away. Folks in the know, say this is indicative of being born with a fully developed 'second sight.'

Family stories tell that Mother was known for having saved more than one life because of this gift. The story most repeated in the family tells of her reading tarot cards for a friend living down the block from us when we lived on Liberty Street in Hamilton Township, NJ. I was still a young girl.

In the middle of the reading, she burst out, "Gracie, hurry, hurry, run home, quickly. Your house is on fire!" Indeed it was. The woman's young son was playing with matches and the curtains in the kitchen caught fire. The sleeping baby in the second floor bedroom was safely removed while the neighbors doused the kitchen fire. Fortunately the warning averted what could have been a disaster.

I struggled for years keeping my family together. I raised three children while my husband was in the hospital fighting a terminal disease that took his life after 7 years. Money doesn't come easy when you have no education for a decent job. I love my children, so that made the years of hard work worth it.

27

Like my mother, I also have a highly developed extrasensory perception, but only where my children are concerned. I moved to Florida after my children were grown and out on their own. By that time, my first grandsons were about 3 years and 1 year old. My daughter and I stayed in touch by telephone and by letters and cards—her letters, my telephoning. I don't write. After a few months of being a Floridian, I called her and asked, "Why haven't you told me you're pregnant again?"

"What makes you say that? I don't have any reason to think that I am."

She was. I knew it before she did. She delivered another grandson 9 months later.

It became a tradition for my son Bob to go to his sister's house every Wednesday for supper. One particular Wednesday evening, I called. "What happened? Why didn't you call me? Did Bob have an accident? Is he alright?"

They were relaxing over a cup of coffee after dinner when a loud crash in front of their house had them running to see what happened. Some guy ran into my son's newly acquired and highly treasured Cadillac. He worked hard and long to buy that car. This all happened only 5 minutes before my phone call.

Ten years later, after I was widowed, I returned to New Jersey and moved to Bordentown in the early 1970s with my daughter and four grandsons. My daughter works two jobs to keep the bills paid. She works hard. I keep the house, make dinner, and do the laundry. Our house is old, but it has a nice feeling to it.

My habit is to get up early in the morning to have a cup of coffee and start a load of wash before all the day's commotion begins. One particular morning, the strangest thing happened to me. I didn't want to tell my daughter because I didn't want to frighten her.

As I was bending over the washer, I looked up to see a little girl about 7 or 8 years old standing a good 8 feet from me. She had long blonde hair, curling at the ends. Her little toes peeked out from under her long nightdress and her nightcap had a ruffle on it. She was holding a candle, watching me, but with a pleasant expression on her face. Not smiling, just a contented, sweet look. I was stunned. I stared. I blinked. She was gone.

Audrey's Story

My late husband Wesley and I lived on West Street when our daughter Sherry was born. Soon after, Wesley stopped in at the deli on Farnsworth Avenue where he ran into Lillian. We both have known Lillian all our lives.

"Wesley, do you know of anyone who wants to rent a house?" she asked him. "Yes, me." He replied. And that's how we rented the house that you (talking to the author) bought years later.

Sherry was about a year old, time for her to have her own room, when we moved into the house. She had so many toys that my mother suggested I place half of them in the attic with the idea of switching them every 6 months. Then I would take her up to the third floor and, while I was sorting the toys out, she was playing with this little children's phonograph. Instead of playing a record on it, she took it apart. She loved taking things apart then putting them back together again. Once in a while, she wouldn't be able to find a space for a piece that was supposed to go back in. We always said she was going to be a lady mechanic when she grew up.

One particular day when I was sorting the toys and Sherry was playing quietly, I suddenly felt the hairs on the back of my neck stand up. I felt a presence, standing behind me, looking over my shoulder. Almost like a coolness on my back. I brushed the thought from my head.

"Mommy," Sherry said with a bit of surprise in her voice. "What," I said, lifting my eyes to hers. She said nothing more, but was staring past me, as if she saw someone standing in back of me. I watched her eyes move as though they were following someone moving. But no one except Sherry and me were there.

I didn't say anything to anyone about it. My husband pooh-poohs stories about ghosts or spirits. He just chuckles at me. But then one day, Wesley went into the attic to get something. When he came downstairs he had a funny look on his face. I noticed immediately. "What's wrong?" I said. "Nothing, nothing." He replied. I didn't press it. He would tell me when he was ready.

A week later he said to me, "You know last week when I was in the attic? There's something up there. I could feel this chill down my back, like when you have a fever and a breeze hits you. I could feel it, but I couldn't see anything. There's something in that attic. I know it. There is something there."

I chuckled. Now he believed my stories. There was never anything frightening or scary. But there was definitely a spirit there. It's funny how the non-believers change after they have the experience of a 'happening.'

Not long after the incident in the attic, our family gathered together for a Thanksgiving dinner. An in-law of my sister's, Mrs. B., I called her, told me that two psychics, sisters, lived in that house for 4 years before we moved into it. That same afternoon, Mrs. B. told me the house was haunted. Never anything mean or evil or even bad, she said. "Nice ghosts" is how Mrs. B. referred to the many stories she knew of the house. She died some time ago and took her stories of the house with her. But not before she told us 'things' happened downstairs too.

We wanted to buy that house, but we just weren't ready when it was available. I loved that house. Thirty years later, I learned that others experienced 'something' in the same house. (Note: See Author's Story and Mom's Story.)

Years after we left there, Wesley and I bought a house of our own. Sherry came in one day and said, "Dad, did you start to paint the back porch steps?"

"No, I will eventually, but haven't had time to start any repairs yet."

"Well, come here. Someone must have started to paint them red. Why would anyone paint steps bright red?"

We all saw it. It wasn't really like anyone took a brush to it, more like a splash of red. Then we thought no more about it. A couple of days later, I went out to hang clothes on the line. I didn't notice any difference on the way out because I was carrying the clothesbasket. However, on the way back into the house, I noticed the step was clean. Wesley must have found something to clean the paint off, I thought.

Wesley came home for lunch and I asked him, "What did you use to get the paint off the steps?"

"I haven't touched the steps, yet. I haven't had time. Why?"

It was gone. The steps were clean. The stain was gone.

When Sherry came over. I showed it to her.

"Daddy's playing a trick on us," she said. "The steps are immaculate."

He swore he didn't.

Six months later, it was back. The bright red stain was back. In the exact same place. This time when friends came to visit, we showed the spot to them so they wouldn't think we were kooks. Then it disappeared. But later it came back again. I suggested painting the steps, maybe a different color. Sherry got a bad feeling about that. "Please don't do that, Mom."

So I didn't. We never did find out what it was.

After Wesley died, I put the house up for sale. In the meantime, I rented the house out to a couple with a teenage daughter. I told them my husband was very sick there just before he died. Some people are squeamish about those things, so I told them right up front. They lived there for a short while when they called me. "Did Wesley work at night?'

"No," I told them. "He worked for the city, daylight hours, 7:30 to 4:00."

"Every night at 10:30 on the dot, I hear what sounds like a lunch pail being dropped onto the table. I thought it was your husband. His ghost is in this house. I feel he is still in this house."

They also heard noises coming from the semi-detached house next door. A family lived there for a while. Then it became empty. They insisted the noises continued after the house became vacant. They even checked to be sure no one was camping out in there illegally.

My father, Warren, was psychic, too. He was ill with Parkinson's disease in his later years. During the week, I drove my daughter to school, then I went to visit Dad and help my mother with him. She had a bad knee and couldn't do it all herself. On a day when I was needed for some extra activity in Sherry's schoolroom, I telephoned Mom not to expect me. I would be spending the day at school. I didn't want my father to be disappointed waiting for me when I wasn't going to be there. When my mother tried to tell him not to expect me, he insisted that I would come to visit.

"Tiny's going to be here, Mabel, you'll see. She's going to call. You'll see." She got out of patience with him when he kept insisting. Well, my job at school didn't take very long after all, so I telephoned to say I was on my way. "I told you Mabel," he said.

He often sensed just before the phone would ring. And it would. Mother used to marvel at it. I can do that too. Sense when the telephone is going to ring. I don't know how, I just know.

Sherry's Story

When my husband and I bought this old historic house, it had been vacant for a few years. It took some time, but we did major repairing and restoring before moving into it in September. I love this house. We intend this to be our home for life.

I came over one sunny afternoon with Saylor, our year old, black cocker spaniel and Lhasa apso mix. She's just a bouncy, happy, frisky pup, always looking for attention and willing to play. Men were still working on the house, but this afternoon no one else was here. I wanted to decide how to finish the bookcases in the dining room. I was pondering the situation when I heard someone jog down the stairs in a light-hearted way. The sound was that of hard-soled shoes, almost making a clacking noise as they descended. The sound stopped at the last step. Saylor scooted over to the bottom of the stairs in a flash. She immediately lay on her back like she was expecting a 'belly-rub.' The hairs stood up on the back of my neck. I was stunned, unnerved, I grabbed her leash and left without another thought about the bookcases.

Real estate is my profession. Since we were going to live in an historic house, a house with a closed-up tunnel entrance in the basement, I did a little research on the background. Prince Lucien Murat and his wife (nee), Caroline Georgina Fraser, lived here in the early 1800s. The prince was a son of Napoleon and Joseph Bonaparte's sister Caroline. Joseph Bonaparte owned Pointe

Breeze, the estate right up the road from here. Tunnels were dug from his palatial home to the Crosswicks Creek and to his daughter Zenaide's lake house. We wonder if our tunnel was connected in some way.

Eventually, after the prince spent all of his wife's fortune, Madame Murat and her two sisters, Jane and Eliza Fraser, opened a day and boarding school for young ladies here. Presently, it is called Murat Row, at that time it was called "Linden Hall." They developed a very successful school for young ladies. The school was highly acclaimed with a waiting list for enrollees. Of course, the girls were all taught music appreciation and the playing of instruments, including the flute. It seems people wanted their daughters to be socially trained by a real princess.

The prince was passionate about dogs and horses. He imported many different breeds of dogs and took extremely good care of them. The way Saylor reacted that day assured me, whoever bounced down those stairs, must have loved dogs.

Saylor used his dog crate in our former house. In our new house, he enjoyed running through the rooms so much while we were renovating that after we actually moved in, we just continued to let him run loose. We latched the door shut on his crate and took it up to the third floor with other storage boxes. During the night, we awoke to hear the crate door being opened, closed, opened, closed, back and forth several times. The next morning, we went up to check. The door was latched tight just as we originally placed it there.

Even now that we've been in the house for a while, when the house is very quiet, Saylor will lift his head and look around as if he is acknowledging someone's presence. He sees someone that we don't. We're delighted that our resident spirit seems to be a happy, contented one. Not like an earlier experience.

The realtor I worked for at the time was taking a group of us to tour a house we recently listed for sale. When we came to one area of the basement, I began to suffocate. I couldn't breathe. I got out of there as fast as I could. It didn't seem to bother anyone else. Later, I was told that area of the basement held the coal bin and someone had been buried alive during the delivery of a ton of coal. Having psychic abilities is not always pleasant.

This ability goes back as far as I can remember and farther. When I was a toddler, we lived in the same house you, (the author), later bought. My mother says I often 'saw' someone in the attic while we were up there sorting toys. She never did see what I was seeing.

Paul's Story
(Refers to previous story)

My wife Sherry plays the flute. She's been studying for some time now. I enjoy listening to her practice and recognize melodies, but not the titles of the songs she plays. I'm a light sleeper, Sherry isn't. In the middle of the night, I awoke to the beautiful melody of the flute. The sounds floated through the air. It was familiar and I knew it was classical, but couldn't tell you the name of the song. I kept hoping Sherry would wake up to hear and identify the music. But I didn't want to move lest I would frighten the spirit away and the playing would cease. It was very peaceful.

Author's Note: Murat Row has long been divided into several independently owned houses.

Bruce's Story

In the early 1970s, I purchased an old row house in the historical City of Bordentown with my then wife. The house dates to the early 1800s.

Shortly after moving into the house, we acquired two cats. The cats would make a practice of playing at the foot of the stairs. They would leave their toys in the same spot, right at the foot of that staircase. Always.

I thought little of this until one day I saw one of the cats playing in their favorite spot. She was leaping high into the air and flipping around, behavior I had never seen before, even with all the cats my family had when I was a child.

Later, my wife said she saw a small 'sparkling cloud' come down the stairs and stop at that same spot where the cats played and left their toys. She believed that this was the ghost of a child. I never saw it and I don't believe she ever saw it again.

Sometime after that, my wife, some friends, and I began experimenting with a Ouija® board in our living room. One night, we attempted to contact any spirits that were available. We began to get responses very quickly from a 'spirit' who started out by communicating, "Help me. Mommy, help me" and "hurts" over and over again. When asked whom we had contacted, the response was 'no one.' We tried to ask the 'spirit' questions, but had difficulty getting beyond those few statements. It felt like we were talking to a child. The 'spirit' eventually did reveal that his name was, I thought, Jacobs. I seem to remember that it was a boy's first name, but am no longer certain. The child related that he died of cholera in 1848.

Author's Notes: Ouija® was acknowledged in Rome and Greece even before the time of Christ, though in various designs. The Ouija® board was first brought to the American public as a parlor game over a hundred years ago. Many people who believe in the occult will use the board to contact 'spirits' as a form of channeling. One variation of the board has a moveable three-legged device that points to the numbers, letters, or words yes, no, or maybe on the board in answer to the question asked. A minimum of two people must be present, but a third to record the answers is suggested. Many people regard the Ouija® board mere amusement, while others give it full respect and honor its answers.

Four thousand Irishmen were brought into New Jersey to build the D & R Canal with picks and shovels, in the early 1830s. Locke number one was two blocks away from this house. When the epidemic of Asiatic cholera hit this area, the stricken men digging the canal were buried where they dropped, along the banks of the canal. The disease is transmitted by water. It killed 2000 people in 1832 in this country.

Cholera is a terrible disease that begins with cramps in the fingers and toes then attacks the extremities. It is very painful. The skin on the face takes on a brownish color, coldness takes over the body, and the pulse becomes weaker until it is no longer discernable. The voice fades to a whisper as thirst increases, sweats break out, and the body goes into an irreversible coma. Cholera was still causing occasional deaths in this area in the 1840s.

Further information: Captain Fraser built this house (now divided into several privately owned homes) for his daughter Caroline. She eloped with Prince Lucien Murat, the nephew of Joseph and Napoleon Bonaparte. Joseph became a resident of Bordentown in the early 1800s with the plan of bringing Napoleon here also. The Bonaparte estate was called Pointe Breeze. The prince found his way to Bordentown and stayed several years after Joseph returned to Europe to gather his family together.

The prince was a loveable spendthrift. He happily wasted his wife's wealth quickly and poorly invested the inheritance of her sisters. As a result, she and her sisters developed and very successfully turned the house into a finishing school, Linden Hall, for young ladies.

By 1848, the Bonaparte family again raised its power and wealth in Europe. Murat left Bordentown to secure his inheritance. With that accomplished, he sent for his wife, three sons, and two daughters, never to return to Bordentown again. They did leave a young son buried in Christ Church graveyard.

Could this be the spirit of the Murat child, feeling deserted by his family in 1848? Or could this be the spirit of a child born of a canal builder wandering the neighborhood looking for the comfort of a mother long gone?

Betty's Story

I was sitting with Betty in the living room of the Victorian house she bought a few years ago. This is the third house in Bordentown she has owned since I first came to know her in the early 1970s. It has a wide, side-entry hallway with a door on the right that leads into the living room. There is also a door that opens to a formal dining room behind it. To the left of the dining room is the kitchen, now very modernized by Betty's talented sons. The house is at least a hundred years old. The former owner was a highly respected scholar and genealogist.

Betty is a very creative, talented person who ran a women's casual clothing store, a tailor shop, and gave sewing lessons. Her business, the Pincushion, was located on the main street in this old historic town. She would often be working there from 10:00 in the morning until after midnight.
This is her story.

"When I had the shop on Farnsworth Avenue, I was so overloaded with work between my sewing class, running the store, and doing alterations that I asked Linda to come to work for me. Shortly afterward 'things' began to happen.

Items were moved, lost, and then found in obvious places. I would be working at cutting out a pattern, lay my scissors down, get up to go to the bathroom, return, and the scissors would be gone. I would

47

get a cup of coffee, return to my seat, and the scissors would be lying there.

Or Linda, my assistant, and I would be sewing late at night, get up to make a pot of coffee, and come back to our worktable to find the spool of thread I was using could not be found anywhere. Linda affectionately referred to the little events as 'Martha's doings.'

Martha was playful. She was never destructive. When she moved an item I was using, it would be found easily. It was as if she just wanted some attention paid to her.

The time came when I had the opportunity to sell my house and my commercial building on Farnsworth Avenue to move to this house, still in Bordentown City, where I could combine both. I jumped at the idea. Once I made the decision, things went quickly. The last night before the big move, I was alone in my shop thinking about this big change in my life. With change, there is always adjustment. I couldn't go without considering my spirit friend. So, I extended the invitation.

"Martha, it's time to go. You can stay here with the building if you like, or you can come with me."

At this point, Betty got up to make a fresh pot of coffee. Soon I could smell that wonderful aroma wafting in from the kitchen as the sound of coffee percolating filled the quiet moment. She returned and continued with her tale.

"I settled into my new home, set up my sewing shop in the large finished basement. Soon buttons left lying on the sewing table would be found under the cabinet. A yard of delicate, pink silk material necessary to finish a dress I was working on would be stuck in between bolts of navy blue wool. I knew, then, that Martha had chosen to come with me. During a quiet moment when I was working alone, I heard the sound of a woman's light step walking overhead in the hallway. No one else was in the house at the time. It was kind of reassuring to have Martha with me.

While our renovation was in progress, my son David was laying concrete in another section of the basement. He was troweling the floor, sprinkling it with water, troweling, etc. He reached for the trowel, that quick, it was gone! Martha was obviously back to her old tricks and having some fun. He looked around and found it on the windowsill behind some bottles."

Betty went to the kitchen to pour some coffee for us.

Returning to the room she said, "The coffeepot was turned off, but it's still hot. I think Martha wants us to know she is here.

Once I searched for an entire week for a jar of salve left in the sewing room before I found it on the second level of the house under the computer. Sometimes while I'm watching television, I'll hear *whoosh*! Down the hallway toward the kitchen, *whoosh*! I know it is Martha having fun in the hallway racing around.

I've never really seen her. Once, my friend Maria came to visit. We both fell asleep while watching a TV program. Suddenly, I awoke hearing a noise in the kitchen. I slowly crept to the dark hallway, down the hall, and reached the darkened kitchen. Carefully, I slipped my hand around the corner, flipped on the light switch. No one was there. But the disposal unit was going full force and the switch was still in the 'off' position."

Old Ironsides' Story

He has been seen walking along the edge of his property, where the Delaware River slaps against the shore, on many nights when the moon is full. Walking slowly, thoughtfully, with his head bent down to meet his hand rising up. Walking alone.

Charles Stewart, born in 1776 of Scottish and English royal ancestry, joined a ship as a cabin boy when he was 13 years old. By the time he was 22, he was master of his own merchant ship. Next, the American Navy enticed him with the second highest rank on ship, a lieutenant. Then he became a Master Commandant. His daring actions in the rescue of a party of ladies during an uprising of slaves in the West Indies were noticed and brought to the attention of the King of Spain. His position in the American Navy made him unable to legally receive gifts from other countries, so he accepted a personal gift from the King—a finely-crafted sword created especially for him that he carried throughout his life.

As Commander of the USS Constitution during the War of 1812, his performance was exemplary. Soon he was appointed Commodore, the highest rank in the American Navy at the time.

The beautiful young Delia Tudor of Boston, Massachusetts' society came into his life. They married in 1803—a marriage that produced two children, Charles and Delia, and near disaster for the Commodore.

He bought the Bordentown estate of Francois Frederici in 1816—a mansion the General of Surinam built in 1797. The property sat on a high bluff, bordering and overlooking the Delaware River. He named it Montpellier, but everyone else affectionately called it 'Old Ironsides.'

The command of the entire Pacific on the USS Franklin was his from 1820 to 1824. At this time, women, by law, were not allowed to leave port aboard ship. Top officers, who sometimes brought their wives, daughters and, on occasion, their friends, on long voyages mostly ignored this law.

During this time in the Pacific, his wife was aboard ship, illegally, when disaster struck. Delia secretly smuggled the deposed President of Peru on board the ship without her husband's knowledge. An international crisis arose. Commander Stewart was brought up on charges to a court martial. This was a staggering event that marred his brilliant naval career. He resigned his commission, avoiding the court martial, and divorced his wife immediately. She fled to her sister and brother-in-law, the Gardiners at 'The Oaklands.' He removed to his estate in Bordentown, NJ. In time, he received a reprimand for the incident, and then returned as Naval Commissioner in 1830-1832. Next, he moved on to become Commander of the Philadelphia Naval Yard.

The office of the first Commander of the Home Guard was also appointed to him. A candidacy for President of the United States was considered, but never offered. His personal life was considered too wild and his companions undesirable. He retired from the Navy in 1861, but was called to Washington for a consultation by President Lincoln in regards to the firing upon Fort Sumpter. He was 83. Congress promoted him to the newly-established rank of Rear Admiral (retired). In 1864, he was the only surviving officer of either civil or military service of the USA who held a commission granted in the 18th century. The man's career record was brilliant.

He was obviously a man of passion, daring, and adventure. He sailed all over the world, but chose Bordentown as his homeport. Here he was recognized as being a quiet, country gentleman living on his estate with his mistress, a devoted, much younger relative reputed to be a descendent of Field's estate in the neighboring town of White Hill.

Here, his love of children, flowers, birds, and his 'farm' was common knowledge. Here, his daughter and granddaughter, Delia Stewart Parnell and Fanny Parnell (respectively mother and sister of Charles Stewart Parnell, leader of Irish Home Rule in Ireland), also chose as their home. Here, also, Fanny Parnell later became internationally known for her work with the Irish Land League. Here, the famous came to visit and seek advice from the famous Fanny Parnell, herself.

And finally here, after a raging storm, a bird flew in his open window and perched on his bed, filling the room with song as he lay dying. Here, where he found peace from his battles, Rear Admiral Charles Stewart is seen from time to time in the dark of the evening. Walking along the edge of his property, where his land and the Delaware River slap together like his professional and his private life. Walking under the full moon. Walking alone.

Gladys' Story

Florence became a bride at the approximate age of 40. Her new husband Cornelius built a house especially for her. She lived there among her many antiques for 54 years, surpassing her husband's death in 1953. Uncle Charlie worked for Florence for many of those years. Having no heirs and no relatives when she died, she left the house she loved and all the contents to Uncle Charlie. He didn't want to live alone, so he invited my family and me to share the house with him. We all delighted in our new home.

Uncle Charlie and I were always very close. We had a special bond between us. As a child, I helped him by pulling weeds, carrying the ashes to the curb, and other small chores that would lighten his workload a bit. After we settled in, I continued our old routines. In the spring and fall of every year, we went into the attic and brought down the change of curtains, bed linens, etc., for the oncoming season. Uncle Charlie showed me exactly how he liked things done. I, as always, would go along and just do things his way. I also took on the housekeeping. When I ran the vacuum in the living room, I picked up gray hairpins. The next day when I ran the vacuum again, gray hairpins would be at the same place. None of us in the house had gray hair, so I was curious how they got on the carpet.

My daughter Gay chose Florence's former bedroom as her own because it was near the bathroom. "Mom, it's the strangest thing. I wake up and hear sounds of someone brushing their teeth." (After Florence broke her hip she always brushed her teeth in bed.) "I hear a voice in the bathroom saying, 'I just don't understand. I just don't understand.' The voice sounds very dazed like the person is confused."

Time passed, the children grew, Uncle Charlie died. He, in turn, left the house he loved to the family he loved.

After we buried Uncle Charlie, I soon noticed the fan-backed Windsor chair that stood near the doorway to the kitchen was turned to an angle. I straightened it to face the living room. In the morning, it was turned again and, again, I would straighten it. In the morning, the chair faced the wrong way again. This little ritual went on for about 10 days until the chair finally stayed where I placed it.

About 3 weeks after Uncle Charlie was buried, Gay came home from a date with her eventually-to-be husband. Just inside the doorway they heard, "I'm in here Gay. I'm in here." It was Uncle Charlie's voice just as clear as when he was alive and called to her in the same exact way.

When it came time to do the semi-annual visit to the attic, I asked my husband to help in Uncle Charlie's place. I planned to continue the routine Uncle Charlie set so many years ago. While sorting out the curtains we heard, "Over here, Gladie, over here." Uncle Charlie was there just as he always had been, calling his favorite person by her pet name. But that was the last time. He must have moved on after he saw me doing things the same way he taught me.

We never heard from him or Florence again.

Lois's Story

We have lived here for over 30 'odd' years. Odd, at times, for sure. But the family never had any fear in living here. It has been a comfortable home to all of the three generations of my family. But there were times when, well, I'll just tell you the stories.

My daughters Beth and Andrea were blamed more than once for things they just didn't do. When my girls were both still less than 8 years old, their grandmother hollered up the stairs to their bedroom on the second floor in the back of the house.

"Stop that dancing around and making such a racket!" I'd yell up the stairs to them. There was no response, so I finally went up the stairs and down the hall to reinforce my mother-in-law's wish, and my two young girls were both in a deep, sound sleep. They looked like angels. Silence filled the room. No signs of anything astray. Or of anyone else being there.

During these growing-up years, Andrea and Beth would often feel 'a *cold whoosh*' of air go past them. This happened in different areas of the house, not necessarily in any particular spot. But in one location in the girls' shared bedroom, they saw an illuminated glow of a man's face on the wall. They weren't frightened. By the time this happened, he was familiar and they were accustomed to his antics. They named him Andy.

It never occurred to any of us to be afraid. Our ghost was never harmful. Mischievous, at times, yes. Items in the house would disappear, then reappear, sometimes in the same place. Sometimes we would find it in another part of the house. The girls would be accused, but often they would be in school or outside the house playing with friends.

One time my husband and I were watching TV in our room at the top of the stairs on the second floor. A sound louder than the program we were watching was the sound of firm, heavy footsteps coming down the hall to our door. Then they stopped. I got up, went to the door, and opened it, not a soul was in sight.

In later years when Andrea became a young woman, she was watching TV in the living room when tables started to move and bounce around. Annoyed, she yelled –"Andy! Get out of here, out, out!" The front door flew open and *whoosh*! Silence. After that day, there never was another problem in this house. Never another thing out of order. Unexplained footsteps were no longer heard. No loud noises rang throughout the house when no one was there. The house became normal and dull without the unknown guest that lived with us for so long.

Kathy's Story

My husband and I came into possession of this big Victorian house about 1986. It's a quiet neighborhood on a high rise above the place where Crosswicks Creek and Black's Creek enter the Delaware River. The street ends at the corner of our property. The house itself dates back to the 1800s.

Soon after moving into our new home, we heard noises. It sounded as if someone was rapping on an outside back door, wanting to enter. We looked, but no one was there. What really confused us was the location of the knocking sounds. There wasn't even a door there. However, there was a large floor-to-ceiling window like the one in the front of the house. After researching the history of the house, we found that where the window is now had once been a large, wooden back door.

My husband Sam had four antique lead toy soldiers. He placed them on the mantel of the fireplace in the music room. One by one, they were beheaded. He found them still standing upright with their heads broken off and placed neatly at their feet. After the third beheading and absolutely no explanation for it, he placed the remaining soldier in the china cabinet in the dining room. This soldier's head remained where it belonged. On his shoulders!

The treasured collector's plates in the same china cabinet were all lined up to face the room. These would be turned sideways. Never broken or chipped. Just turned sideways as if they had been placed differently in another time, in another cabinet. Time and again my husband would turn them to face the room, time and again they would be turned sideways.

When we first moved into the house, we brought a lovely grandmother's clock with us. It had been a family heirloom and had always kept perfect time. It stopped the day we moved into the house. A repairman got it working again. As soon as the man walked out the front door, the clock stopped again. It hasn't worked since.

In time, our foster daughter, Alicia, a teenager, came to live with us. She chose the third floor as her room for the privacy teenagers seek. Soon after, she would hear footsteps come up the stairs, across the hall, and down the stairs. No one was ever there. Many times, she would be the only one at home, no one else would be in the house. Yet the footsteps persisted.

One evening after dinner, Alicia and Sam were in the living room, I was in the kitchen cleaning up the dinner dishes. Lovely concerto sounds permeated the air. We all ran for the music room to see who was the accomplished pianist. The room was empty. The music ceased as soon as we reached the doorway.

Finally, Dec. 25, Christmas evening, after a long day of family reunions and visiting, we came home to quietly enjoy our own living room. Just the two of us looking forward to a quiet hour or two. But not for long. As we sat down to relax, we heard sounds coming from the dining room. Glasses clinking, laughter, music, the sounds of someone giving a dinner party. When we went to the doorway of the dining room, we found silence. Not a soul, not a sound, not a movement.

These occurrences and many others took place in the first 4 years that we owned the house. In the fifth year, we had a daughter, Mary Beth. Since that time, there has been little activity. But the clock still doesn't work.

Pete's Story
(Refers to previous story)

One afternoon, a woman I've never seen before walked into my place, Shoppe 202 Antiques on Farnsworth Avenue. As often happens in small town shopping, she got into a conversation with me. She began telling me about her dreams.

"I see a grand house in Bordentown. Horse-drawn carriages pull up in front of a mansion. Ladies and gentlemen very elegantly dressed step out and enter the house. There are a great many dinner parties. Music floats through the air."

I showed her a stack of Bordentown prints I have for sale. She looked through them until she came to Kathy's mansion, "This is it! This is the house I've been dreaming about!"

I sent her down to talk to Arlene (the author).

Author's note: She repeated her conversation with Pete, to me, and then continued with her background. "My great-grandmother was a cook at the Bordentown Military Institute. I've heard stories about Bordentown all my life, but this is the first time I have ever been here."

Phil's Story

We were very excited when, many years ago, my wife and I bought our house. Wanting to move our possessions into the house in an orderly manner, we laid our carpets down first. Our oriental carpet went into the living room in front of the fireplace. As we began to bring in the furniture, I noticed a neatly placed pile of ashes on top of the oriental carpet. It seemed strange, but I cleaned it up and continued to move the furniture into the house.

I placed a heavy, cherry wood chair in the living room. Before I came back, the chair was very neatly turned over on its side. The pile of ashes was back on top of the oriental carpet. Hmm. Something odd here. But I was too busy moving our things in to pay too much attention.

After we settled in, my wife and I were often awakened at midnight by a tinkling of a bell that was sitting in our china closet. The cherry wood chair was often turned over on its side. We never heard a clunk of the chaired being turned over, but it would still be turned over all the same.

Then in the middle of one night, I awoke to a heavy weight on my chest. My wife kind of pooh-poohed my comments. The next night it happened to her.

We called in a parapsychologist. He explained to us. "It sounds like you have poltergeist activity. This means physical materials are moved by mental thoughts. It is not always intentional. Stress, hormonal peaks, and mental turmoil create the situation. Often a teenager will subconsciously act as a magnet, especially if they are stressed. They do this subconsciously, completely unaware that the happenings are being caused by them. Females seem to be more susceptible at this age than males.

This is called psychokinesis or PK for short. It is the ability to bend spoons, cause dishes to fly across the room with no apparent reason, levitate a glass of water, etc. Many studies have been conducted on intentional PK. In case of poltergeist activity, it is unintentional.

You have a teen-age daughter in the house. She is probably under stress with the moving into a new neighborhood. With time, caring, and understanding, the activity will cease."

It did.

Printed in the United States
64137LVS00002B/157-171